THE
FIELD & STREAM
Fish Finding Handbook

The *Field & Stream* Fishing and Hunting Library

FISHING

The Field & Stream *Baits and Rigs Handbook* by C. Boyd Pfeiffer

The Field & Stream *Bass Fishing Handbook* by Mark Sosin and Bill Dance

The Field & Stream *Fish Finding Handbook* by Leonard M. Wright Jr.

The Field & Stream *Fishing Knots Handbook* by Peter Owen

The Field & Stream *Fly Fishing Handbook* by Leonard M. Wright Jr.

The Field & Stream *Tackle Care and Repair Handbook* by C. Boyd Pfeiffer

FORTHCOMING TITLES

HUNTING

The Field & Stream *Bow Hunting Handbook* by Bob Robb

The Field & Stream *Deer Hunting Handbook* by Jerome B. Robinson

The Field & Stream *Firearms Safety Handbook* by Doug Painter

The Field & Stream *Shooting Sports Handbook* by Thomas McIntyre

The Field & Stream *Turkey Hunting Handbook* by Philip Bourjaily

The Field & Stream *Upland Bird Hunting Handbook* by Bill Tarrant

THE
FIELD&STREAM
Fish Finding
Handbook

Leonard M. Wright Jr.

Illustrations by Rod Walinchus and Richard Ellis

THE LYONS PRESS

An earlier version of this book was published in 1978 by New Century Publishers under the title *Winchester Press Fish-Finding Guide*.

First Lyons Press edition—1999

Printed in the United States of America

10 9 8 7 6 5 4 3 2 1

Library of Congress Cataloging-in-Publication Data

Wright, Leonard M.
    [Where the fish are]
    The Field & stream fish finding handbook / Leonard M. Wright, Jr.
; illustrations by Rod Walinchus and Richard Ellis. — 1st Lyons Press ed.
        p.   cm. —(The Field & stream fishing and hunting library)
    Originally published in two editions: Where the fish are. New York
: Times Books, c1978 and Winchester Press fish finding guide.
Piscataway, N.J. : New Century Pub., c1978.
    Includes index.
    ISBN 1-55821-896-3
    1. Fishing.   I. Field & stream.   II. Title.   III. Title: Field
and stream fish finding handbook.   IV. Title: Fish finding handbook.
V. Series.
SH441.W74   1999
799.1—dc21   98-50024
                                                            CIP

Contents

Preface

NINETY PERCENT of your fishing problems are solved once you have discovered *where the fish are.*

Admittedly, you will not catch much when fishing the hottest trout spot in the river with a 12-inch striped bass plug. Nor can you expect to take many stripers with a gnat-sized trout dry fly. But even a beginner using any commonsense bait or lure over a concentration of fish will catch more than the expert casting over barren water.

And that is what this book is designed to do—to put you on top of the most fish, in most places, most of the time.

Suppose you are a saltwater angler who finds himself on a large, unfamiliar lake. Or suppose you are an expert stream fisherman visiting the seashore for the first time. Finding the fishy spots in the thousands of acres of water in front of you will probably seem as impossible as finding a needle in a haystack.

Not so. Almost all fish have predictable habits and habitats. Fish are utterly selfish and self-indulgent. They want either the most food, the most comfort, or the most safety. Where they find all three together, they'll stack up like cordwood.

The preferred foods of the more common fresh- and saltwater fish are given on pages 46 through 58 and 97 through 112. So are their comfort requirements—their tolerance to currents, temperature preferences, and types of bottom or shelter they seek. The safety factor is more complicated because it varies widely from species to species and from situation to situation. However, you will find many clues on places where fish feel secure scattered throughout the many "where-to" and "when-to" pages in the four major sections of the book.

Let us go back to that unfamiliar lake, for example. The first thing you have to find out is *what kind* of fish are in it. You may know from hearsay that it's largemouth bass and bluegill water. If not, any local

resident or any hardware store, tackle store, or boat livery proprietor
will tell you what species of fish to expect and what they usually
catch them on. If, indeed, the answer is largemouths and bluegills,
turn to pages 48 and 53 for a quick look into the private lives of
these two species. Now suppose again you decide to try for the
larger of these two fish, the largemouth. You now know it prefers
warmish water of medium to shallow depth, likes sheltering weeds,
logs, or snags, and has a yen for minnows, frogs, and crawfish.

Your next step is to leaf through pages 25 to 43 on ponds and
lakes to learn how to "read" the vast expanse of flat water in front of
you. Choose the likeliest nearby place (say, that shallow cove on page
33) and begin fishing a bait or lure that closely resembles a favorite
largemouth food and fish it at a depth and with the behavior typical
of that type of food.

It's as simple as that.

The most successful fishermen are invariably those who can pin-
point fish-producing areas *before* they start fishing. They don't trust
to trial and error. They concentrate their efforts where the fish are.

The following pages are designed to give you—in a few minutes—
what it could take you a lifetime to learn the hard way.

FRESH WATER

Brooks, Streams, and Rivers

R UNNING WATER differs from still water in one important way:
It brings the food to the fish like an endless belt conveyor,
while lake or pond fish have to cruise around and find their
meals. As a result, most fish in flowing water tend to stay in or near
one chosen place for days, weeks, even months, because their food
travels to them.

3

However, most fish make short trips several times a day from their secure resting places to areas where food is more plentiful. These journeys may be only several feet and are seldom more than 100 yards. Then, too, most river fish move slightly upstream as the season advances, seeking temperatures more to their liking. Running water not only gets bigger as it progresses downstream; it gets warmer, too.

Most river fish stake out a territory and defend it from all smaller or weaker rivals. Despite this, fish are constantly seeking to better their lot, and steadily challenge their betters for choicer quarters. So if you catch a good trout, for example, from a deep cut under a root tangle one evening, fish it carefully on your next outing. Another good fish is almost certain to move into this choice vacancy—often within a few hours.

Fish living in running water are usually somewhat smaller than specimens of the same species that inhabit lakes and ponds. Floods and droughts reduce their food supplies. And it takes energy that would otherwise go into growth to battle the current. But river fish undergo tougher training and usually fight harder than their still-water brethren. And perhaps even more important, there's a special charm to flowing-water fishing that has convinced many anglers that this is the choicest fishing of all.

1. OUTSIDES OF BENDS

Wherever running water changes direction, both the main thread of the current and the deeper water will be near the outside edge of the turn. This concentration of food-carrying current, plus the security of deeper water, make the outsides of bends prime fish-holding places.

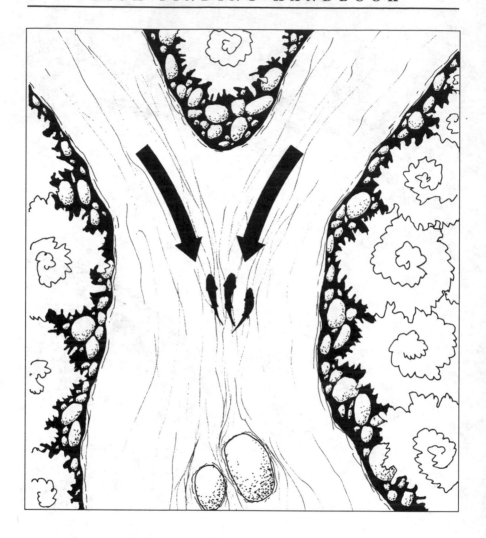

2. MERGING CURRENTS

Where two currents come together, twice as much food is carried to the fish. Wherever you find this condition, along with reasonable depth or protective cover, you will also find fish. In fact, fish often feed at shallow current junctions when they feel protected by the dim light of dawn or dusk.

3. DROP-OFFS

Where water suddenly deepens—as at the heads of most pools—the current slows down and the food carried by the flow begins to settle to the bottom, making easy pickings for fish. Such places have everything: easy food, the safety of depth, and the comfort of a moderate current.

4. EDDIES

Water rushing into a pool faster than it can escape tends to form a large, slow whirlpool. Fish will often position themselves where the upstream flow starts to slow down as well as in the main downstream current. Again, they have the benefits of food, comfort, and safety.

5. DAMS AND FALLS

In places where water drops vertically over an obstruction, it digs a deep, safe hole for fish. In addition, such places are difficult for fish to climb over, so that fish moving gradually upstream to cooler water or to spawn tend to bunch up just below dams and falls.

6. Big Rocks and Boulders

Not only do these break the current—giving fish resting places—but there are also deep holes just below them and often undercuts on their sides. Both of these offer fish safety. Places studded with big rock slabs and boulders are always prime sections of any stream.

7. OVERHANGING BUSHES OR TREES

Since most river fish's enemies attack from above, the fish prefer some overhead cover. Then, too, overhanging foliage or deadfalls give shade as well as protection—a condition most fish seek on bright, sunny days. Even where the water may appear shallow, such places are always worth trying.

8. Undercuts

Another, and often more productive, form of cover is created where
currents undercut banks or rock ledges. Such places, especially cuts
under the roots of big, bankside trees, are the safest of all in the river.
The biggest fish like to take over these lairs and repel all intruders.

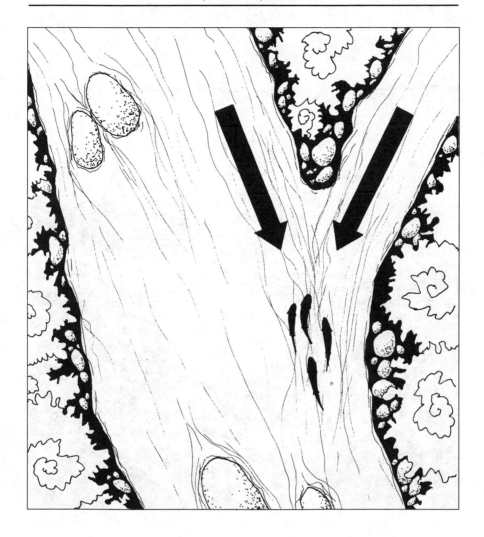

9. FEEDER BROOKS

The junction of a small stream with a larger one is often a top spot—provided there's reasonable depth and cover nearby. Here, not only do you have the advantage of two currents funneling food to the fish, but you also have the cooler water to attract fish in hot summer weather.

10. SPRINGS

Not all additions to streams come from visible brooks. In some places, water wells up into the stream from underground sources. Again, the fish-comfort factor comes into play. Such water is much cooler than river water in midsummer, yet warmer in winter and in early spring.

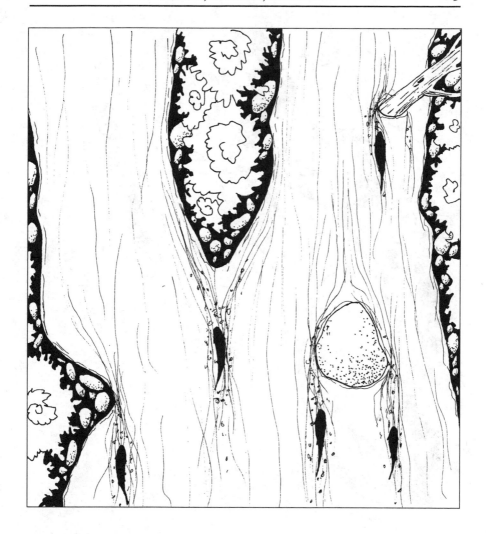

11. Current Edges

Wherever a rock, small island, piece of debris, or any other object pokes through the surface or out into the flow, a short drift line is created. You can often spot them by lines of drift matter or bubbles. Given enough depth or nearby cover, fish will work these natural food funnels.

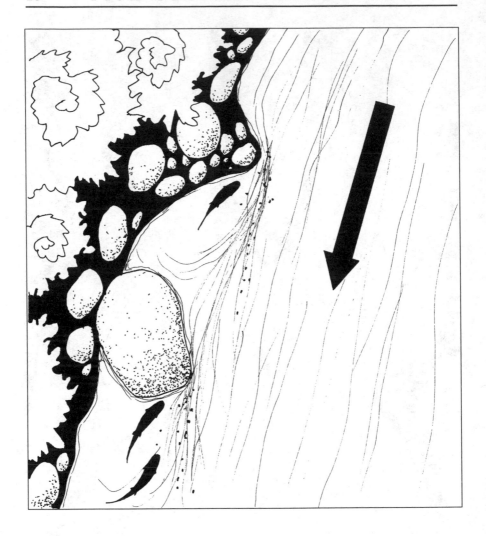

12. MINI EDDIES

Shoreline clumps of sedge grass, rocks, and small indentations in cliff faces create small eddies downstream that break the current and collect food. Fish often hang out in such places for both comfort and food. Such places can be hard to spot, but keep your eyes open for them.

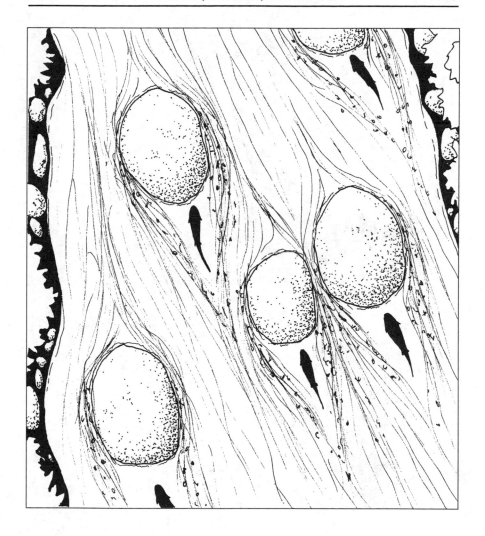

13. POCKETS

Large rocks or boulders emerging, or almost emerging, from rapids cause the current to dig downstream holes, creating mini pools. These can be surprisingly productive, despite their small size—especially during midday or in hot weather.

14. SHADY SPOTS

On summer afternoons, when the rest of the river seems dead, you can often get interesting fishing early in the afternoon by fishing north-south sections with high, shading hills to the west of them. By using a map or by exploring, you can often find such sections and extend your fishing day.

15. TAILS OF POOLS

Late in the evening, often just before it gets too dark to see, fish will drift down the pool and feed at the lip where it breaks out into the next rapids. This is seldom a good location early in the day, but it can offer the best sport of the day on a late-summer evening.

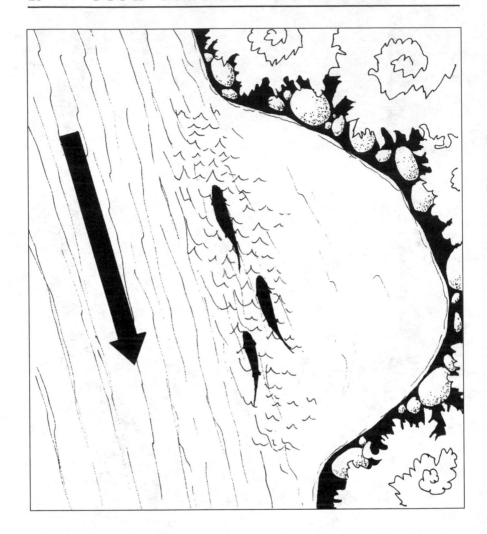

16. DANCING PYRAMIDS

Where slow water meets fast, a series of small, stationary, dancing waves will occur. Food drops to the bottom here, and large, lazy fish will take over these patches—if there's enough depth. Even if depth and cover are lacking, fish are still likely to feed in such places at dusk.

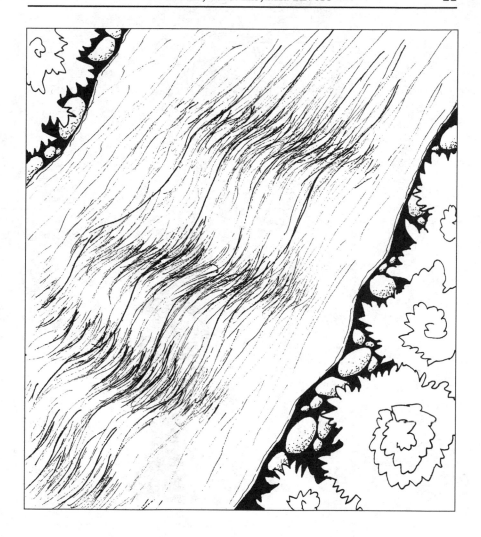

17. Standing Waves

When you see one or a series of stationary "bumps" or waves in a fast run or a rapid, you can be sure there's an obstruction—probably a submerged boulder—directly upstream. Trout, especially rainbows, like such lies—so give them extra attention.

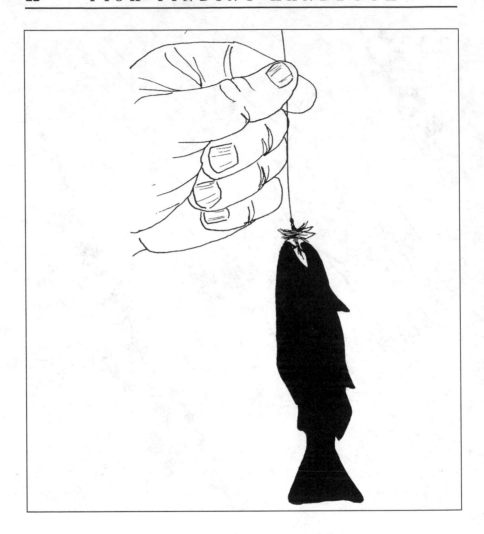

18. LITTLE FISH

If you take a small fish from a place that looks like a choice big-fish spot, move on. Something's wrong. The place just isn't as good as it looks. There are probably no big fish there, because large specimens do not allow small ones within 5 or 10 feet of their lies.

19. Check It Out

During midday—especially on warm, sunny days—it pays to walk through water you expect to fish that evening. You will discover fish lies you would never have noticed by looking at the surface. If you wade in swimming trunks, you can feel the colder water from springs, too.

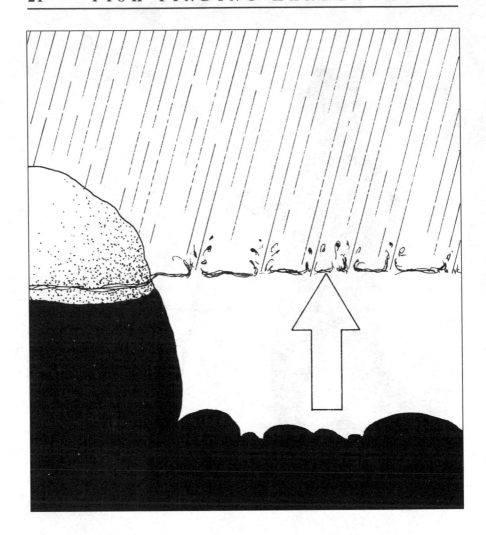

20. RISING WATER

Many streams and rivers seem to go dead during low water and hot weather. However, if you time your trip to arrive right after a good rain when the water is rising and cooling, you can often enjoy fishing that rivals the best you had in springtime.

CHAPTER 2

Ponds and Lakes

S TILL WATERS are harder to "read" than flowing waters. There are
no telltale currents to help you discover where the food is concentrated. Then, too, lakes and ponds are usually quite deep,
making it harder to pick out fish-holding places.

Another problem is that since there are no currents to bring food to the fish, still-water species have to cruise around to find food, and moving targets are notoriously harder to hit. Therefore, it's particularly important to learn all you can about the habits and habitat preferences of the type of fish you are after. You will find the vital statistics on the most popular freshwater fish on pages 44 through 58.

The majority of still-water fish, like the smallmouth bass, feed in fairly shallow water early and late in the day, retreating to deeper water as the sun and temperature get higher. Some, like pike and pickerel, spend most of their time hiding in the shallows waiting for their prey to come to them. And a few members of the trout family spend most of the summer in the cool depths feeding on schools of deep-water baitfish.

The successful pond and lake fisherman, no matter where he travels, is the one who knows the territorial and temperature preference of the fish he's after, figures in the time of day or year, and, above all, uses his eyes. There are always a surprising number of clues to show him the secrets of the flat and baffling sheet of water in front of him. You will find some of the most important of these on the following pages.

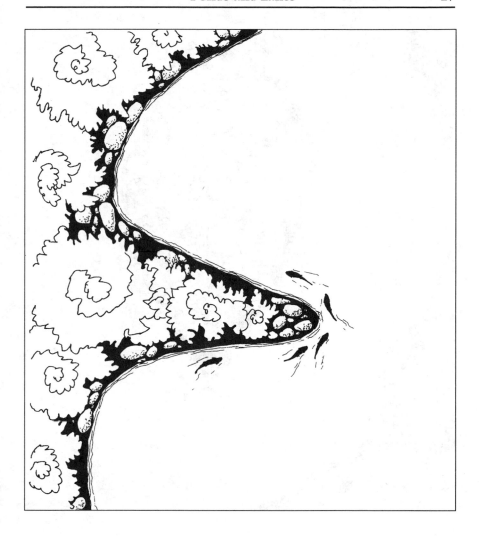

1. Points of Land

A peninsula jutting into the water offers you two benefits. First, it gives you larger areas of the depth that fish prefer along both of its sides. Second, and equally important, fish cruising the shoreline will tend to pass through a small area off the underwater tip.

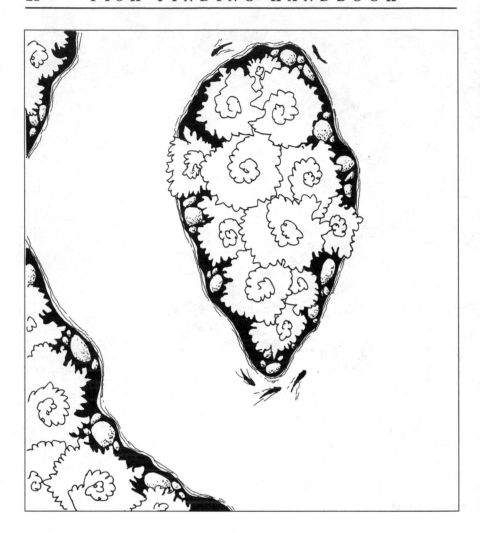

2. Islands

Like points of land, islands give you increased areas of fish-holding and fish-feeding territory. Fish tend to remain near such places in good quantities. Clues to underwater contours and depths are given by the above-water terrain as described in other parts of this section.

3. Cliffs

Like steep banks, cliffs tell you to expect deep water below them. And one thing more: It is also fairly certain that pieces of rock have crumbled off the cliff over the years, building up a productive area of rubble and boulders along the bottom.

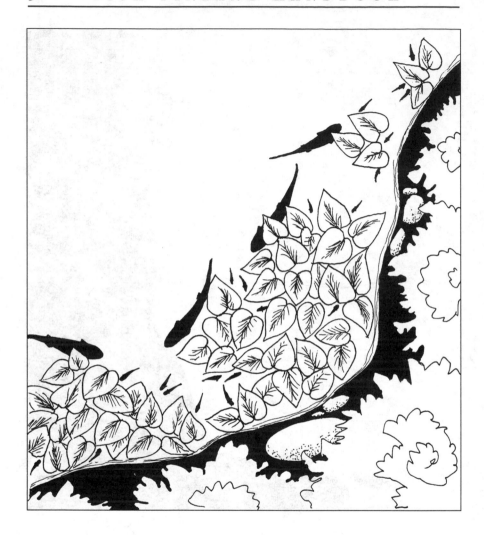

4. Edges of Pads

Small fish, which feed on the insects that live on stems of lily pads and weeds, attract hungry big fish. The shade created by dense patches of pads is also an attraction. Fish along the outside edges and in the larger openings so your line will not get fouled so often.

5. UNDERWATER WEED BEDS

Shallow weed beds can often be seen below the surface; deeper ones have to be located by trolling. Weeds give food and protection to small fish that are sought after by big predators like pike and bass. Work weed beds carefully and thoroughly—especially the edges.

6. Drift Lines

On windy days, you will often notice distinct lines on the water's surface. These are caused by fast-drifting surface water, and are most often downwind—sometimes extending several hundred yards—from points or islands. The surface food concentrated in these lines attracts fish.

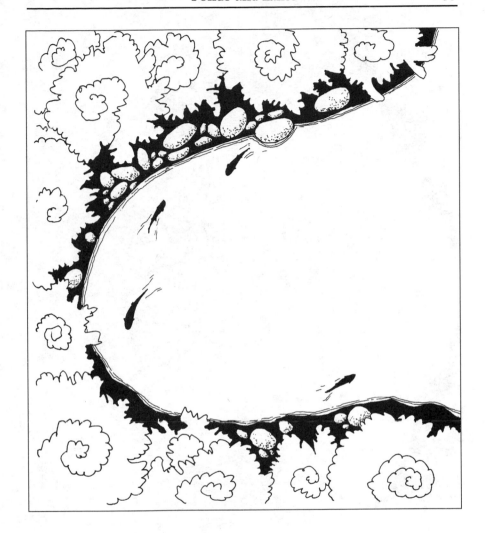

7. COVES

With their long shorelines, extensive shallows, and protection from most winds and waves, coves are top food-producing areas. Shallow sections should produce warm-water fish, and the deep water off the points is a good bet for big fish waiting to make nightly raids for food.

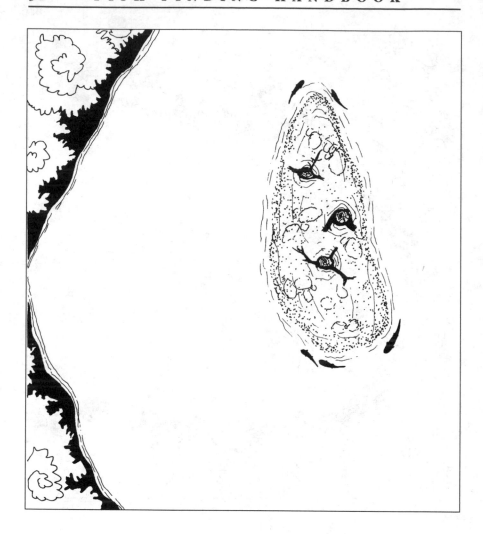

8. SUNKEN ISLANDS

Reefs and underwater bars are really islands that did not quite make it. They offer the same fishing advantages as true islands and should get extra attention. Some are marked by buoys. Others can be found on charts or by searching on sunny, windless days.

9. SPRING HOLES

Where cool water boils up from the bottom, it will attract deep-water
fish during the summer—even if the depth is not great. Such places
are usually well-kept local secrets, but you may find some by testing
temperatures while swimming or by exploring with a mask.

10. Inlet Streams

Inflowing water brings extra food, but just the flow itself seems to attract some fish. Many species, such as smelt in the spring and trout and salmon in the fall, spawn in running water; look for concentrations at stream mouths in the appropriate seasons.

11. STEEP BANKS

Where the land pitches steeply into the water, you can expect good depth very close to shore. Fish that prefer deep water, or those driven deep by summer heat, are likely to be in such places. Various depths along the slope should be tested carefully for different species of fish.

12. GRADUAL SHORES

Where the land slopes gently into the water, look for shallows well out into the lake. Such water, especially if the bottom is sandy, is often unproductive. But if there are boulders or weed beds, give them extra attention, for they may hold most of the fish in that area.

13. BAITFISH

You will often notice that schools of minnows, small sunfish, or perch tend to hang out in a certain area. Big fish that like to feed on them may not be nearby during the bright hours of the day, but be sure to fish such areas carefully at both dawn and dusk.

14. BOULDERS

Big, roundish underwater rocks—especially those over a yard in diameter—provide shade and hiding places for fish both large and small. Crawfish like such places, too. Fish every sunken boulder carefully and, if you find a cluster of them, you have hit a hot spot.

15. Deeper Does It

If you are fishing what appear to be the best places and still are not catching any fish, try farther out from shore. The fish are usually deeper, rather than shallower, than you would expect—especially at midday or during summer, when the surface water gets hot.

16. TRY NIGHTS

During midsummer, when most vacations take place, fish often bite poorly. If working deeper, cooler water does not produce, try fishing at night. This tactic can be especially effective with largemouth and smallmouth bass. Surface lures are usually best.

17. GET A FISH'S-EYE VIEW

It's a smart idea to explore a clear-water lake or pond with swimsuit and mask at midday during warm weather. You will not only locate some unnoticed sunken weed beds, reefs, rocks, and drop-offs, but you are also apt to spot many fish for a later try.

3

Some Popular
Freshwater Fish

BEFORE YOU LOOK through the pictures and vital statistics on
some of the more common inland species, you should know
how the rating system works.

Size: "Small" does not necessarily mean that the specimen you
catch will be bait sized. Brown trout have been classified as small, for
example, because the majority of the fish taken by anglers will weigh
under 1 pound—even though the world record is over 40 pounds.
Similarly, you may take a ½-pound muskellunge even though the average is over 10 pounds.

The simple rating system we have adopted for this book is that if
the average specimen is under 1 pound, the fish is classified as *small*.
If from 1 pound to 7, it is rated *medium*. If it commonly exceeds 7
pounds, we call it *large*.

Range: We have listed the areas where each fish is commonly, but
not exclusively, found. Many species have been transplanted to non-
native areas. Then, too, some cold-water species are occasionally
found far south of their usual range due either to extremely high alti-
tudes or to exceptionally low temperatures created in the tailraces of
deep impoundments.

Depth: This should be interpreted as meaning the usual depth the
fish prefers under summer conditions when most fishing is done. Of
course, all fish in streams live at quite shallow depths, so these are
still-water ratings.

Granted, some species like trout and landlocked salmon may be
caught in the shallows or at the surface very early or very late in the
season. But during most of the fishing season, they will be in relatively
deep, cool water, and their rating reflects this habit. And that is why our
next heading is so important.

Temperature: We have listed here the temperature F. (Fahrenheit) at which each species feeds most actively. Of course, many fish like perch and pike are caught through the ice when temperatures are in the 30s. Our rating should tell you the temperature (and therefore depth) fish will seek as surface waters heat up.

Habitat: Some fish have pronounced choices for placcs to lie or feed. Pike and pickerel love weeds, for example. Others such as perch and landlocked salmon tend to wander all over a lake at a certain depth and are much harder for the angler to locate.

Food: Since most fish live on insects and even smaller food when they are fry, this heading needs some qualification also. The items listed are those preferred by adults of catchable size and are given in the order of their importance.

In short, this section is meant to give you the most helpful information in the shortest form. It is not intended as a definitive work on the lifestyles and habits of these species.

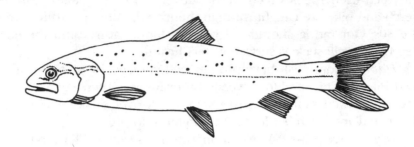

ATLANTIC SALMON (Large)

Range:	Eastern Canada
Depth:	Shallow
Temperature:	Cool, 50s, 60s
Habitat:	Runs and pools
Food:	Small fish

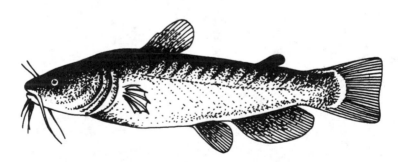

BLACK BULLHEAD (Small)

Range:	Eastern half of U.S.
Depth:	Shallow, medium
Temperature:	Warm, 70s
Habitat:	Muddy bottoms
Food:	Insects, minnows, mollusks

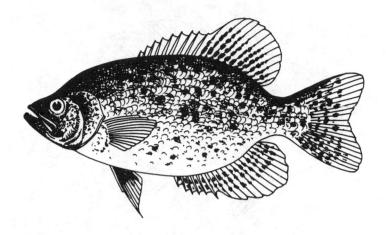

BLACK CRAPPIE (Small)

Range: Eastern half of U.S.
Depth: Shallow, medium
Temperature: Warm, 70s
Habitat: Grass and weeds
Food: Minnows, insects

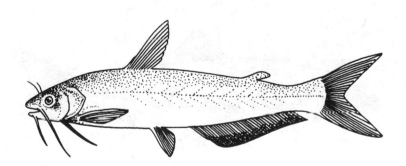

BLUE CATFISH (Large)

Range: Central U.S.
Depth: Shallow
Temperature: Warm, 70s
Habitat: Fast, clear water
Food: Fish, crawfish

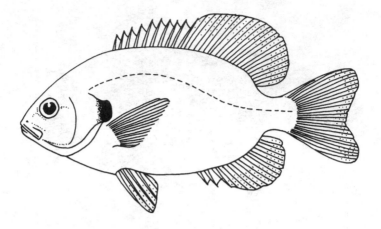

BLUEGILL (Small)

Range:	All of U.S., southern Canada
Depth:	Shallow to medium
Temperature:	Warm, 70s
Habitat:	Rocks, weeds, docks
Food:	Insects, very small minnows

BROOK TROUT (Small)

Range:	Eastern U.S., Canada
Depth:	Medium, deep in lakes
Temperature:	Cool, 50s
Habitat:	Wanders
Food:	Insects, minnows

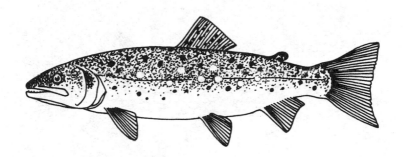

BROWN TROUT (Small)

Range: Northern U.S.
Depth: Medium, deep in lakes
Temperature: Medium, cool, 50s, 60s
Habitat: Near cover in streams
Food: Insects, minnows

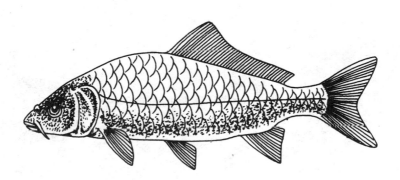

CARP (Medium, Large)

Range: Introduced, entire U.S.
Depth: Shallow
Temperature: Warm, 70s, 80s
Habitat: Mud and weeds
Food: Vegetation, insects

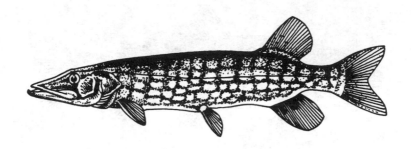

CHAIN PICKEREL (Medium)

Range:	Eastern U.S., southern Canada
Depth:	Shallow
Temperature:	Medium, 60s
Habitat:	Weeds and lily pads
Food:	Minnows, small fish

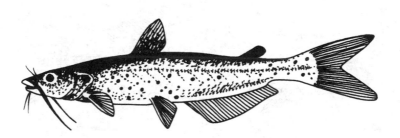

CHANNEL CATFISH (Medium, Large)

Range:	Eastern half of U.S.
Depth:	Shallow
Temperature:	Warm, 70s
Habitat:	Large rivers
Food:	Fish, crawfish

CUTTHROAT TROUT (Small, Medium)

Range: Pacific watershed
Depth: Medium
Temperature: Cool, 50s
Habitat: Brooks, rivers, lakes
Food: Insects, minnows

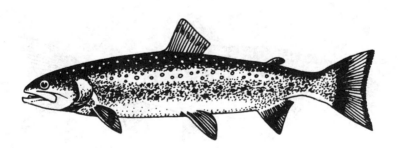

DOLLY VARDEN (Medium, Large)

Range: West Coast drainage
Depth: Deep
Temperature: Cool, medium, 50s, 60s
Habitat: Deep lakes, streams
Food: Minnows, insects

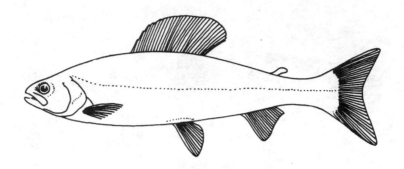

GRAYLING (Small, Medium)

Range: Alaska, western Canada
Depth: Near surface
Temperature: Cold, 40s, 50s
Habitat: Wanders
Food: Insects

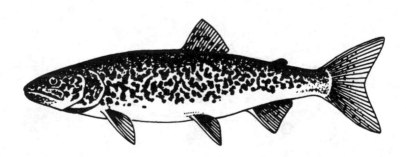

LAKE TROUT (Large)

Range: Northernmost U.S., Canada
Depth: Deep
Temperature: Cold, 40s, 50s
Habitat: Wanders
Food: Minnows, small fish

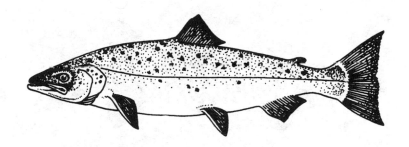

LANDLOCKED SALMON (Medium)

Range: Northeastern U.S., southern Canada
Depth: Deep
Temperature: Cold, 40s, 50s
Habitat: Wanders
Food: Minnows, insects

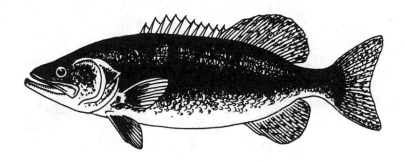

LARGEMOUTH BASS (Medium)

Range: All of U.S., southern Canada
Depth: Shallow to medium
Temperature: Warm, 70s
Habitat: Weed beds, boulders, snags
Food: Minnows, crawfish, frogs

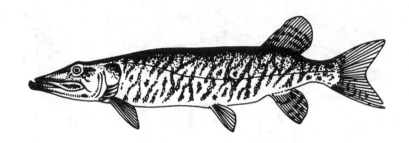

MUSKELLUNGE (Large)

Range: Northern U.S., southern Canada
Depth: Medium
Temperature: Medium, 60s
Habitat: Weeds and snags
Food: Good-sized fish

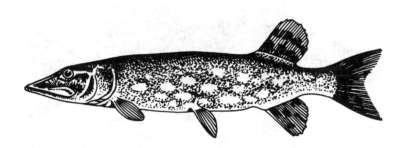

NORTHERN PIKE (Large)

Range: Northern U.S., Canada
Depth: Shallow to medium
Temperature: Medium, 60s
Habitat: Weed beds, snags
Food: Small to medium fish

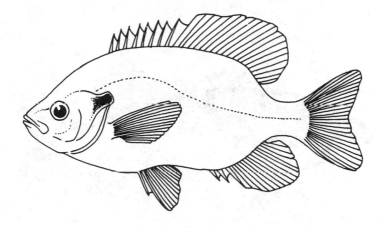

PUMPKINSEED (Small)

Range: Most of U.S., southern Canada
Depth: Shallow
Temperature: Warm, 70s
Habitat: Weed beds, docks, logs
Food: Insects, small mollusks, fish

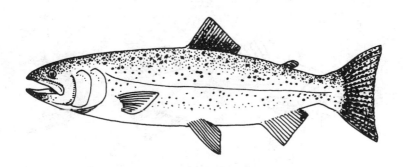

RAINBOW TROUT (Small, Medium)

Range: Northern U.S.
Depth: Medium, deep in lakes
Temperature: Medium, cool, 50s, 60s
Habitat: Wanders
Food: Insects, minnows

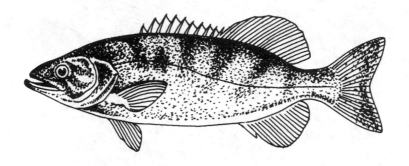

SMALLMOUTH BASS (Medium)

Range: Northern U.S., southern Canada
Depth: Shallow, medium
Temperature: Medium, 60s
Habitat: Near rocks, rocky bottoms
Food: Crawfish, minnows, insects

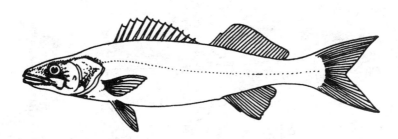

WALLEYE (Medium)

Range: Northern U.S., southern Canada
Depth: Medium to deep
Temperature: Medium, 60s
Habitat: Wanders considerably
Food: Large minnows

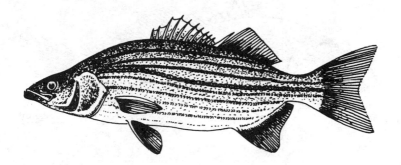

WHITE BASS (Small, Medium)

Range: Central U.S.

Depth: Shallow in evening

Temperature: Warm, 70s

Habitat: Wanders in schools

Food: Minnows, insects

WHITE CRAPPIE (Small, Medium)

Range: Central U.S.

Depth: Medium

Temperature: Warm, 70s

Habitat: Sunken brush

Food: Minnows, insects

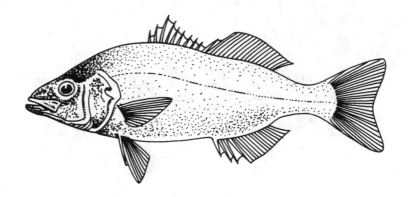

WHITE PERCH (Small)

Range:	Northeastern U.S.
Depth:	Medium, deep
Temperature:	Medium, 60s
Habitat:	Mud bottom
Food:	Insects, crustaceans

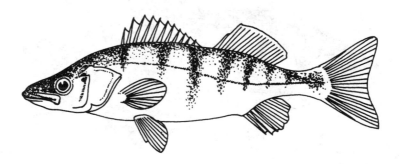

YELLOW PERCH (Small)

Range:	Eastern, central U.S.
Depth:	Medium
Temperature:	Warm, 60–75
Habitat:	Travels in schools over many areas
Food:	Insects, small minnows

SALT WATER

CHAPTER

Bays and Estuaries

T HESE ARE THE areas where fresh and salt water usually meet. Estuaries certainly are a first mixing point of the two types of water; but many, or even most, bays have a touch of freshwater influence.

How does this affect the fishing—and the fishermen? In several ways.

Let us take estuaries first. The strong influence of fresh water here has a great attraction for some fish. Tarpon, snook, striped bass, to name a few, have a well-known urge to enter brackish, or mixed, waters. These waters are also, in spawning season, concentration points for anadromous species: saltwater fish that spend most of their lives in the ocean, but must spawn in sweet water. Some of these are shad, herring, salmon, and sea-run trout.

Surprisingly, some purely freshwater species such as the large-mouth bass can tolerate quite a bit of salt water. There are estuaries in the South where you can catch largemouths and snook on successive casts.

Bays, with or without pronounced freshwater influence, have a few extra things in common. Mainly, they are protected from the ravages of storms and pounding waves. This makes them ideal nurseries for many species of fish and crustaceans—all of which are fodder for bigger and better fish. Also, their shallower waters warm up more quickly in the spring or during summer days, raising the metabolism rate—and feeding needs—of many warm-water species.

By all means, read the next section of this book, "Surf and Shore." A few of the tips in that section can also be helpful to bay and estuary fishermen—and every angler these days needs all the help and advice he can get.

1. NARROWS

Currents speed up where the water is pinched. This digs a deeper channel for fish protection and concentrates the food moving through into a narrower, easier-to-get-at area. Except at dead-high or dead-low tides when water movement ceases, these are hot spots.

2. PIERS AND PILINGS

With their weed attachments they not only provide food for small fish and crabs, but also create protective eddies when currents are running. Small fish plus barnacles, periwinkles, mussels, and oysters that often grow on piers and pilings make these structures choice spots.

3. MOVING PATCHES

Schools of fish like mackerel and a few others can be so tightly
packed that they actually color the water—even when they are a few
feet below the surface. Some baitfish do this also. Always follow and
cast to such places until you are sure your eyes are playing tricks.

4. STRANGE RIPPLES

These can also be created by school fish, but only when they are very close to the surface. Even when the light is bad, you can spot these slight surface disturbances. Ripples can be caused by a school of baitfish or by predators. Get to such suspicious breaks fast and start fishing.

5. BIRDS

Wherever baitfish are pushed to the surface or boil up wounded from deep water, seabirds will gather quickly. Fishermen who follow close behind should do well. If the minnows seem frightened to the surface, fish shallow. If they're boiling up wounded, fish deep.

6. BRACKISH PONDS

These may hold significant quantities of catching-sized fish only occasionally, but they are important as nurseries and as food supplies.
Where they empty into bay, ocean, or tidal river, you can expect fish
to be positioned for easy pickings—especially at low tide.

7. CHANNELS

Fish often follow channels in and out with the tide, not only because the water is deeper, but because the food-bearing currents are stronger. Anchor just off the edge and fish into deeper water. Buoys often mark channels. It's illegal to tie up to them, but smart to fish near them.

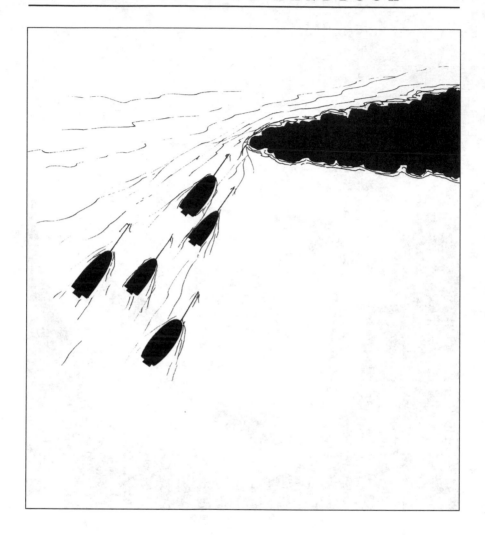

8. OTHER BOATS

One of the surest ways to find good fishing spots is to watch where other boats go. Anglers who fish an area regularly know where the fish are—or where they *usually* are. Nobody can complain if you follow their example. But you can become unpopular if you crowd in too close.

9. BENDS

Tidal rivers, like freshwater rivers, dig deep and tend to undercut their banks on the outside portions of bends. Most food will funnel through such places, and their extra depth and overhead cover make them choice holding places for many types of gamefish.

10. BACKWATERS

Where tidal currents flow in a direction that is opposite to the main flow—as they often will for short distances just below sharp points or obstructions—food will tend to drop to the bottom. Schools of baitfish tend to gather here, attracting bigger predators.

11. JUMPING BAITFISH

Whenever you see a shower of minnows in the air, get to the area and start fishing quickly. Baitfish don't jump because they need the exercise. They arc trying to escape from danger—usually big fish that are lurking below and are actively feeding.

12. SWIRLS

On calm days or in the evening, you will often see a boil or boils on the surface. This usually means that a fish has taken a shrimp, swimming crab, or minnow just below the surface. The bigger the swirl, the bigger the fish, so fish the larger boils first.

13. BAY ENTRANCES

Where bays empty into the ocean—often through a narrow cut or channel—there will be a strong current to pull food in and out, according to the tide. The biggest fish in the bay, including some visitors from the ocean, are likely to hang out here.

14. CHUM

When fishing is poor or slackens off, even though you are in a choice spot, it often pays to try to attract fish and start them feeding again. Extra bait or crushed clams, mussels, crabs, and so on, parceled out downcurrent, will usually start the action.

15. STIR THINGS UP

Even if you have no chum or spare bait aboard, you can often attract fish—especially bottom-feeding types—by dragging your anchor in a small area. This works best over a sand or mud bottom. It uncovers bottom food, and the clouded water itself will usually draw some fish.

Surf and Shore

HERE, YOU ARE on the rim of a vast ocean. There is no influence of fresh water. Nor are the relatively shallow inshore stretches protected from surf or storms.

And this, perhaps, is what makes fishing from beaches and rocky shores so exciting. On all but rare calm days, waves created hundreds, even thousands, of miles away hammer away at the shoreline.

It is the power of these waves that creates a special type of fish feeding. It sets up powerful currents. It churns up the sand temporarily, exposing crabs, sand eels, sand bugs, shrimp, and so on, giving feeding fish sudden targets of opportunity.

Whether you fish from the shore itself or offshore from a boat, there is one important fact to remember. Many types of small fish migrate up the coastline in spring and down again toward warmer water in fall. This creates a "river" of fish—some earlier in the season than others—up and down the coastline for most of the year. Newspaper and radio reports will usually tell you what part of this migration, and how concentrated, is in your area.

The ocean can be dangerous to waders and boaters, so be careful, be watchful, and be prepared. You are trespassing on the edge of an area where even large ships have disappeared. But this is also the place where the biggest fish of all live, and that adds an extra zest to fishing.

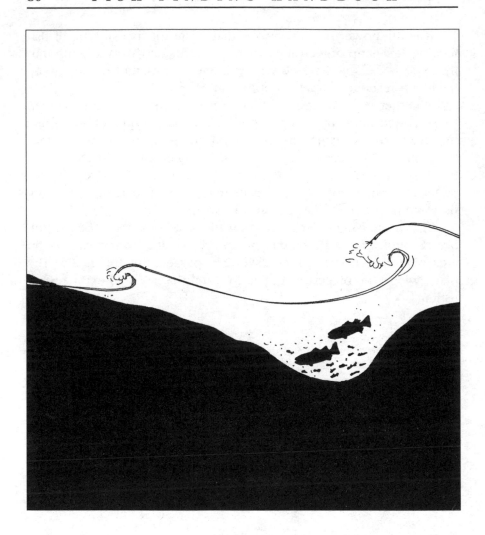

1. OFFSHORE BREAKERS

Where waves break a good distance offshore and there is a relatively calm patch of water between them and shore, you can be sure there is some relatively deep water between the breakers. Here is a natural place for food, baitfish, and gamefish to collect.

2. THROATS OF TIDAL PONDS OR CREEKS

At ebb or low tide, salt creeks and ponds pour strong currents into the ocean—carrying a stream of crabs, shrimp, and minnows with them. At times like these, such places are hot spots, but at a high, or flooding, tide they may provide only so-so fishing.

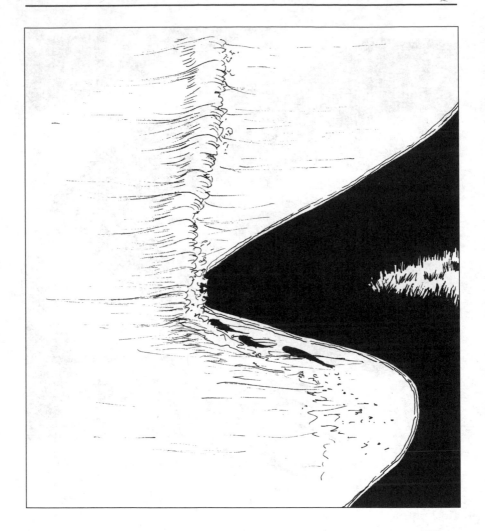

3. POINTS

These are natural fish concentrators because schools, or single fish, cruising the coastlines tend to pass by just off the point. And when tides are running slightly crossways to points, you get an extra bonus: They tend to create big eddies that hold baitfish, drift food, and gamefish.

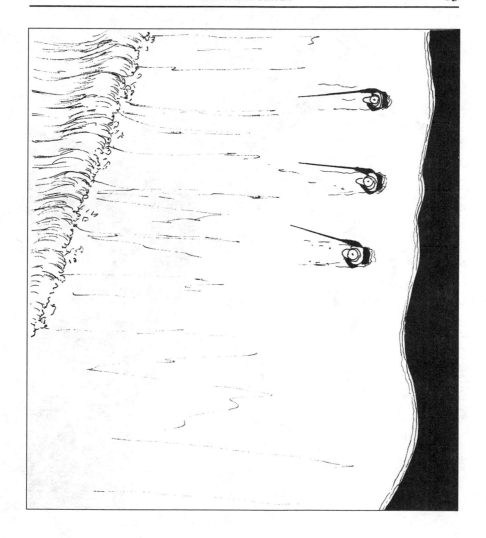

4. OTHER FISHERMEN

Many other fishermen you see are locals with local knowledge and experience. Fish near them (observing a decent interval) or where you have seen them fish, and you will cash in on old-timer's knowledge. (You will also find most of them fishing in places described in this section!)

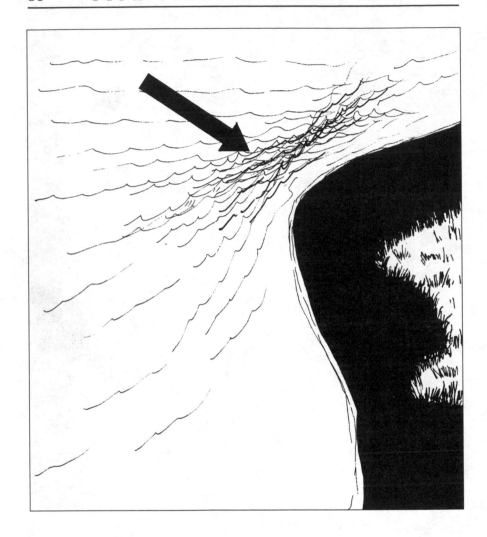

5. DANCING WAVES

Where two currents—even light ones—collide, a stationary patch or strip of small dancing waves will occur. Food will tend to collect or drop to the bottom in such places, attracting feeding or just lazing baitfish, which in turn will attract the hungry predators you are after.

6. DARK PATCHES

These usually mean weed patches or clumps of rocks with weeds attached. Rocks hold crabs, mussels, barnacles, and so on, while weeds offer protection for minnows and other types of food. If there are only a few of these in a sandy area, fish them hard and pay special attention to the edges.

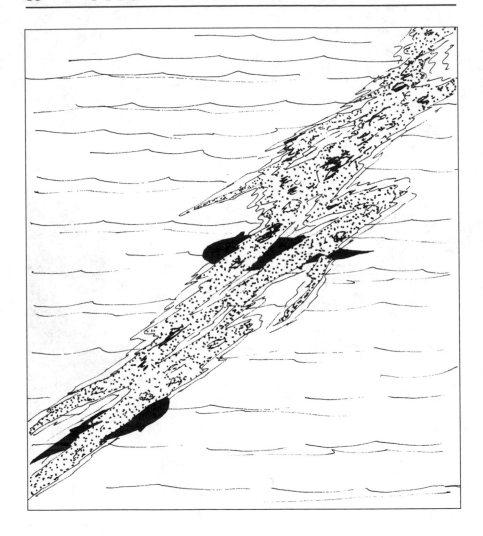

7. LINES OF SPUME OR FLOTSAM

These visible trails usually mean the edge of a tidal current—often one so slight that it leaves no other traces. Debris attracts baitfish and smaller marine organisms. Bigger fish are attracted in turn. And some fish, like dolphinfish, lie in the shade that is created.

8. JETTIES AND BREAKWATERS

These structures not only give shore anglers access to deeper water, but also have special fish-attracting qualities of their own. Their rock structure offers hiding places for crabs and fish, and they create currents and eddies that bunch baitfish and other food.

9. CLIFFS

There are almost always boulders and rock slabs on the ocean bottom below rock cliffs—whether you can see them or not. Years of storms and surf have quarried these from the rock face. Such places are favorite haunts of striped bass, tautog, and many other species.

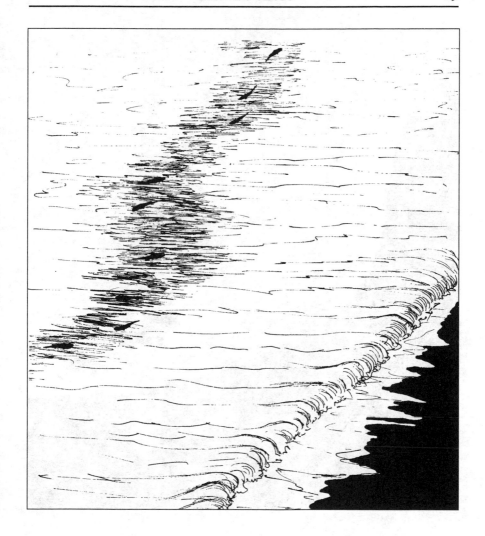

10. DARK WATER

Deep water is a different color from shallow water. It is usually a darker green or deeper blue. Many fish—especially during daylight hours—hang out in deeper water than you would expect, so give the deeps extra attention if the shallows are not producing any action.

11. ROILY WATER

Some portions of the shoreline are more susceptible to erosion than others, and here the surf stirs up bottom silt and food while nearby areas remain clear. Fish the edges, not the centers, of such patches. Fish enjoy the extra food here, but dislike getting sand in their gills.

12. TIDAL RIPS

Points of land, sunken sandbars, underwater channels, and the like can funnel tidal flow into easily seen temporary "rivers." Their faster flow and usually greater depth attract fish looking for either food or safety. Fish find such places quickly, so fish them carefully.

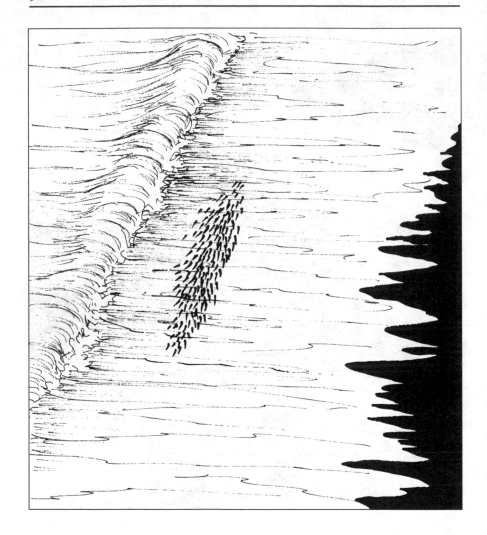

13. BAIT SCHOOLS

Wherever you notice a concentration of small fish—whether in an eddy, off a jetty, or seen through a wave in the surf—cast quickly. Fish eat fish. If you want to do the same, give extra attention and effort to places where bite-sized specimens gather.

14. INCOMING TIDES

If you have a choice of fishing time, take the flood tide. This does not hold true in all situations, but fish usually feel bolder, feed more heavily, and work in closer to shore when the water is getting deeper.

15. TRY NIGHTS

Most hospitable and accessible shorelines attract so many bathers and boaters during the summer that gamefish are commonly driven off into deeper water. All this changes after dark when the crowds are gone. Big fish often raid the shallows for food after dark.

16. AFTER A BLOW

Major storms can often muddy the inshore water so badly that fishing is ruined. But a good blow or mild storm, in most areas, quickens the surf and stirs up extra food. If the water remains reasonably clear, this is a prime time for the surf caster.

Some Popular Saltwater Fish

HERE'S THE RATING SYSTEM we've used for saltwater species.

Size: If the average specimen taken is under 3 pounds, we've labeled it *small*—no matter how large that species may grow. If the average catch is from 3 to 15 pounds, the legend reads *medium.* If commonly over 15 pounds, the species is considered *large.*

Range: Many fish are caught, occasionally, far from where they are expected. The barracuda, a tropical fish, has been reported as far north as Massachusetts, for example, but do not expect many north of Florida. The range given is the area where significant numbers can be expected.

Depth and Range: A fish, like most species of mackerel, may live in deep water but feed mostly in the surface layer. Most flounder, however, live in relatively shallow water, but hug the bottom. Both characteristics are noted where possible.

Some saltwater species, like tautog, have a distinct environmental niche in shallow-to-medium depth around rocks. Others cruise and forage the coastline at various distances from shore. Again, we have tried to tell you as much about these characteristics as possible in a very few words.

Food: Preference is covered as accurately as possible. Some fish, like the snook, live almost entirely on small fish, once they have grown up. Bonefish, however, eat clams, crabs, and shrimp as well as the occasional minnow.

Again, this is not an encyclopedia. It simply tries to give you the most, and most useful, information in the fewest words.

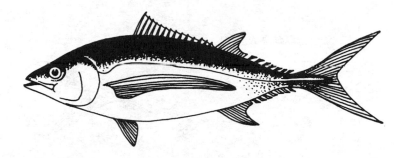

ALBACORE (Medium, Large)

Range:	Atlantic and Pacific Coasts
Depth:	Medium to surface
Habitat:	Wanders in schools
Food:	Small fish, squid

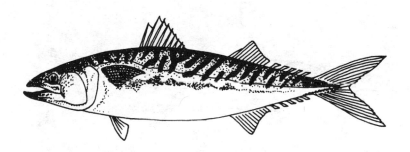

ATLANTIC MACKEREL (Small)

Range:	North Atlantic Coast
Depth:	Surface to medium
Habitat:	Wanders in schools
Food:	Minnows, crustaceans, squid

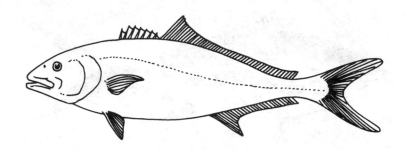

AMBERJACK (Medium, Large)

Range: Southern Atlantic

Depth: Medium

Habitat: Wanders

Food: Small fish

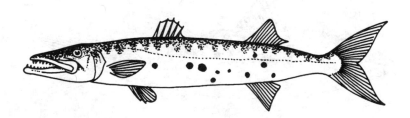

BARRACUDA (Medium, Large)

Range: Tropical, both coasts (several species)

Depth: Near surface

Habitat: Cruises deep-water reefs and
                rocks in shallows

Food: Medium-sized fish

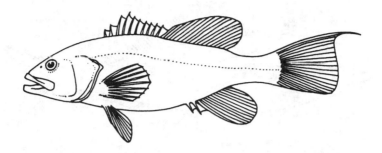

BLACK SEA BASS (Small)

Range: Central Atlantic
Depth: Medium
Habitat: Hard bottoms, wrecks
Food: Mollusks, crabs, minnows

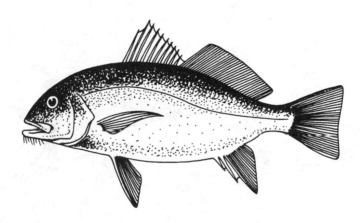

BLACK DRUM (Medium, Large)

Range: Southern Atlantic and Gulf of Mexico
Depth: Shallow
Habitat: Sandy shores, bays
Food: Clams, crabs, shrimp

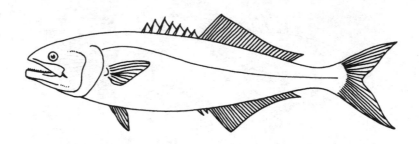

BLUEFISH (Medium)

Range:	Entire Atlantic Coast
Depth:	Medium to surface
Habitat:	Wanders in schools
Food:	Small fish

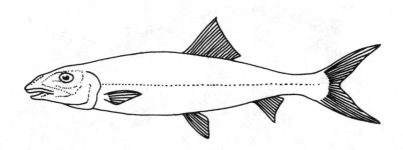

BONEFISH (Small, Medium)

Range:	Florida, Bahamas, and south
Depth:	Very shallow
Habitat:	Sandy or grassy flats
Food:	Clams, crabs, shrimp, minnows

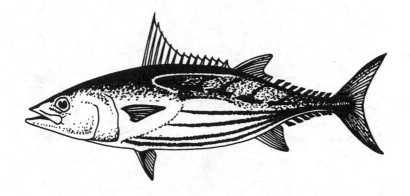

BONITO (Medium)

Range:	Pacific, southern Atlantic
Depth:	Near surface, medium
Habitat:	Wanders in schools
Food:	Small fish

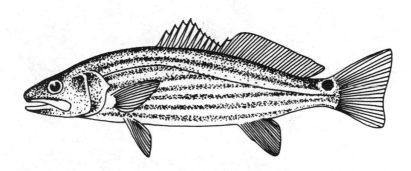

CHANNEL BASS (Medium, Large)

Range:	Southern Atlantic and Gulf of Mexico
Depth:	Shallow
Habitat:	Bottom
Food:	Crustaceans, mollusks, fish

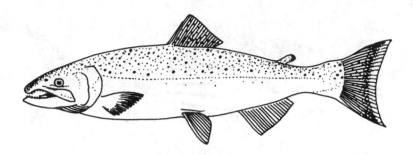

CHINOOK SALMON (Large)

Range: Pacific, California to Alaska
Depth: Medium, deep
Habitat: Bays, estuaries
Food: Small fish

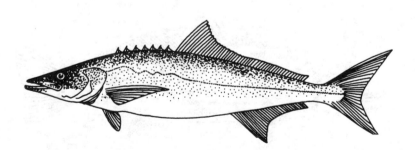

COBIA (Medium, Large)

Range: Southern Atlantic
Depth: Shallow, medium
Habitat: Buoys, pilings, flotsam
Food: Crabs, shrimp, small fish

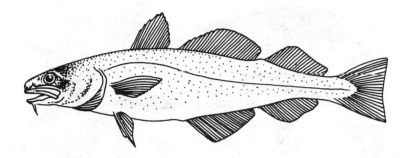

COD (Large)

Range: Northern waters, both coasts
Depth: Bottom, deep water
Habitat: Over banks
Food: Small fish, shellfish

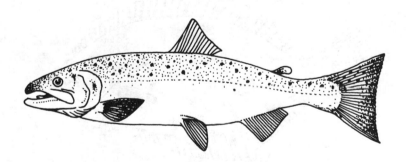

COHO SALMON (Medium, Large)

Range: Pacific Coast, Great Lakes
Depth: Medium
Habitat: Bays, estuaries
Food: Small fish

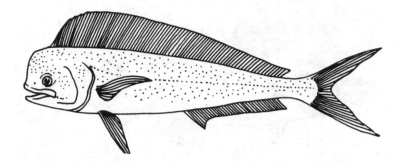

DOLPHINFISH (Medium, Large)

Range: Southern Atlantic
Depth: Near surface
Habitat: Under floating weeds, flotsam
Food: Small fish

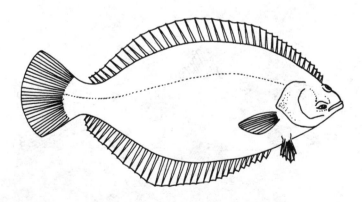

FLOUNDER (Small)

Range: Northern Atlantic Coast
Depth: Shallow
Habitat: Muddy, sandy bottoms
Food: Worms, crabs, shrimp

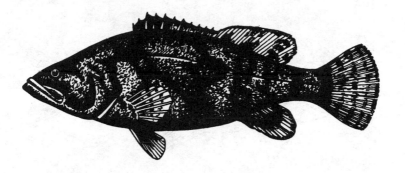

JEWFISH (Large)

Range:	Southern Atlantic
Depth:	Shallow
Habitat:	Coral heads, caves
Food:	Fish

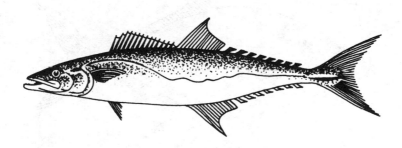

KINGFISH (Medium, Large)

Range:	Southern Atlantic
Depth:	All depths
Habitat:	Wanders in schools
Food:	Shrimp, small fish

POLLACK (Medium)

Range: Northern Atlantic
Depth: Medium
Habitat: Wanders in schools
Food: Small fish, shrimp

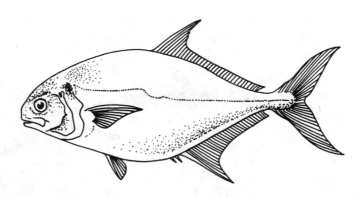

POMPANO (Small)

Range: Southern Atlantic and Gulf of Mexico
Depth: Shallow
Habitat: Sandy beaches, inlets
Food: Shrimp, crabs

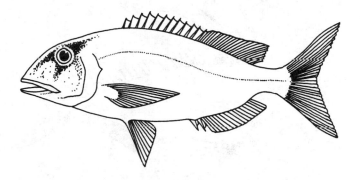

PORGY (Small)

Range:	Northern Atlantic Coast
Depth:	Medium
Habitat:	Bottom
Food:	Small crustaceans, worms

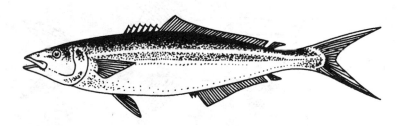

RAINBOW RUNNER (Small, Medium)

Range:	Tropical waters
Depth:	Shallow, medium
Habitat:	Wanders
Food:	Small fish, crustaceans

ROOSTERFISH (Medium, Large)

Range: Southern Pacific
Depth: Shallow, medium
Habitat: Sandy beaches
Food: Small fish

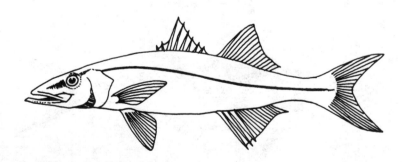

SNOOK (Medium)

Range: Warm Atlantic, Gulf of Mexico, Pacific
Depth: Shallow
Habitat: Brackish bays, rivers
Food: Small fish, crustaceans

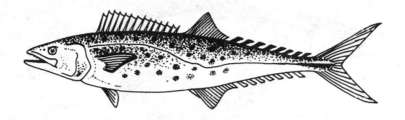

SPANISH MACKEREL (Small, Medium)

Range: Southern Atlantic
Depth: Shallow, medium
Habitat: Wanders
Food: Minnows, shrimp

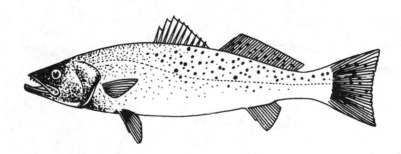

SPOTTED WEAKFISH (Small, Medium)

Range: Southern Atlantic, Gulf of Mexico
Depth: Shallow
Habitat: Weedy bays and tidal rivers
Food: Shrimp, crabs, minnows

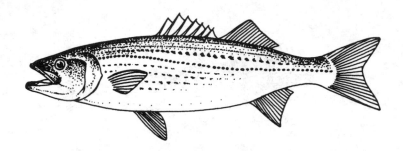

STRIPED BASS (Medium, Large)

Range: Mid-Atlantic, mid-Pacific Coasts
Depth: Shallow, medium
Habitat: Brackish bays, coastlines
Food: Fish, crustaceans, clams

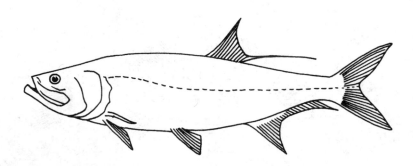

TARPON (Large)

Range: Southern Atlantic Coast
Depth: Shallow
Habitat: Brackish bays, lagoons, rivers
Food: Small fish, crustaceans, shrimp

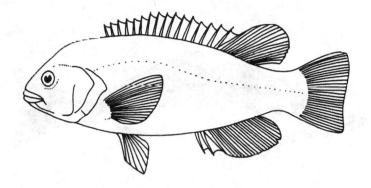

TAUTOG (Small, Medium)

Range:	Northern Atlantic Coast
Depth:	Shallow
Habitat:	Rocks, mussel beds
Food:	Barnacles, mussels, crabs

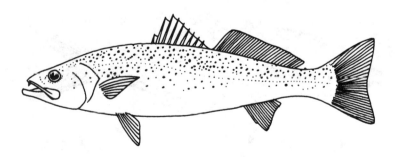

WEAKFISH (Small, Medium)

Range:	Mid-Atlantic Coast
Depth:	Shallow, surface to bottom
Habitat:	Shallow, sandy areas
Food:	Worms, shrimp, crabs, minnows

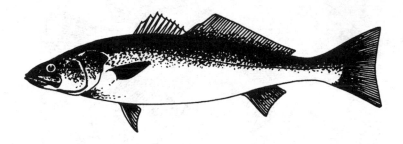

WHITE SEA BASS (Medium, Large)

Range: Central to southern Pacific
Depth: Medium
Habitat: Near kelp beds
Food: Fish, crustaceans, squid

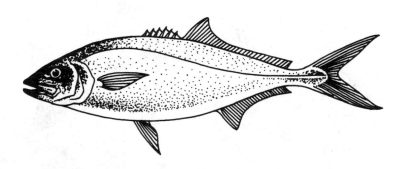

YELLOWTAIL (Medium)

Range: Southern Pacific Coast
Depth: Near surface
Habitat: Wanders in schools
Food: Small fish

HOW TO CARE FOR AND CLEAN YOUR CATCH

Kill your fish (a sharp blow just behind the eyes with a stick will kill most small species), gut it, and remove the gills as soon as possible after you land it, for inner parts spoil quickest. Put it on ice or in a refrigerator as soon as you can. *Do not* leave it in water, even though the water may seem cool.

If you have no ice, keep the fish dry and in the shade. Be sure it gets a good circulation of air around it. (Even with these precautions, fish can spoil in a few hours when the temperature is over 70 degrees F.) Fish, unlike cheese and wine, definitely does *not* improve with age. Unless you are going to freeze or smoke it, the sooner you eat it the better it will taste.

Following are some of the simpler, more popular ways of cleaning fish.

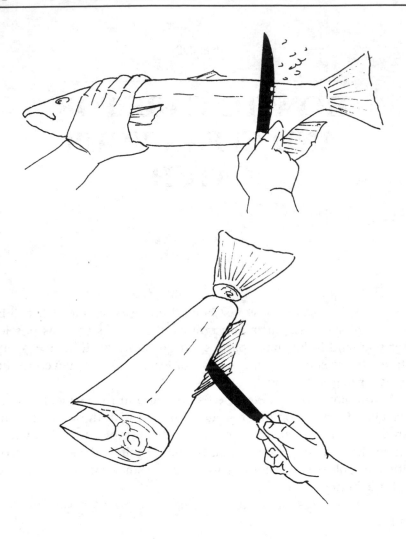

SCALING

This is the easiest way to prepare sunfish, perch, and other panfish for frying. Use a scaler or a sharp knife held perpendicular to the fish and stroke firmly from tail to head. The fresher the fish, the easier the scaling. Run the knife fairly deep along each side of both dorsal and anal fins to pull them free. Finally, slice off the head with a diagonal cut from back of the head down toward the vent and remove the remaining viscera.

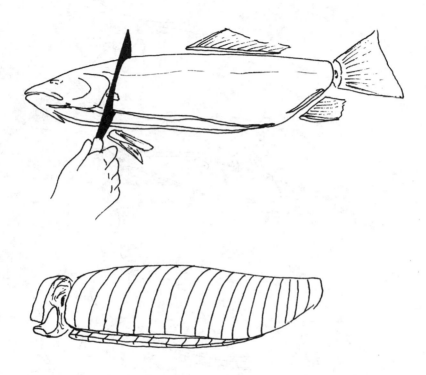

STEAKING

Large fish are often steaked for grilling or broiling. Scale the fish and remove the major fins. Clean out the viscera. Place the fish on a board and, with a sharp knife, cut cross sections of your desired thickness, starting just behind the head and working down toward the tail.

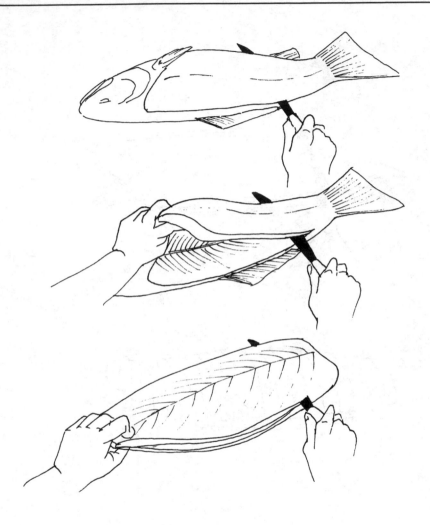

FILLETING

Place the fish on board and cut on an angle just behind the head down to, but not through, the backbone. Slice along the backbone (but not through the rib cage) to a point just behind the vent. Now push the knife through to the opposite side and run it with a sawing motion along the backbone until the flap of flesh is cut free at the tail. If the fish is small, cut off the fillet where the ribs start; if it is large, run the knife down over the rib cage to cut a full fillet.

Lay the fillet skin-side down on a board and, starting at the tail, angle the knife blade toward the skin and work forward until you have freed the fillet from the skin.

Place the fish on the board again and repeat the filleting process on the other side. When you have finished, you will have two boneless, skin-free slabs of flesh.

Filleting is easier if you use a well-sharpened special filleting knife.

Now, enjoy your catch.

Index